No Man's Land

Tupa Snyder

No Man's Land

Shearsman Books
Exeter

First published in in the United Kingdom in 2007 by
Shearsman Books Ltd
58 Velwell Road
Exeter EX4 4LD

www.shearsman.com

ISBN-13   978-1-905700-60-8

ISBN-10   1-905700-60-1

Copyright © Tupa Snyder, 2007.

The right of Tupa Snyder to be identified as the author of this work has been asserted by her in accordance with the Copyrights, Designs and Patents Act of 1988. All rights reserved.

Acknowledgements
My gratitude to Lucia Cordell Getsi and Andy Brown, my mentors, for sharing their experience so generously. Also, for their faith throughout the writing of this first collection. My gratitude also to Tony Frazer, my editor, for devoting so much of his time and insight in nurturing this book through its last revisions.

Some of the poems in *No Man's Land* first appeared in other journals and anthologies, sometimes in earlier versions. They are: 'Behind this Eye,' 'Coalescence,' 'The Kingfisher,' 'Floating,' 'Split,' 'Subtracted Memory' and 'Hover' appeared in *The Allotment: An Anthology of New Lyric Poetry* (Stride Publications, 2006); 'My Father's Crown,' 'When Mother Returns to India', 'Little Death,' 'The Kingfisher' and 'Coalescence' appeared in *The Spoon River Poetry Review* as part of a 'featured poet' selection; 'Echoes in Grey' and 'Shadows' appeared in *Shearsman Magazine*; 'Blue Bill,' 'Vanhorn' and 'Grandma's Death' from 'Split' and 'The Language of Flowers' appeared in *Agenda*; 'Fitting In' appeared in *Succour*; 'Pull' appeared in *Exeter Flying Post*; 'Immigrants' appeared in *Maquette Magazine*.

The publisher gratefully acknowledges financial assistance from Arts Council England with its 2005-2007 publishing programme.

Contents

India from the Raj Bungalow
    The Kingfisher   13
    Hover   14
    Coalescence   15
    My Father's Crown   17
    Behind this Eye   24
    Shining Diamond   28
    Subtracted Memory   29
    Little Death   31

In the New World
    Immigrants   35
    Split   36
    Bluebill   40
    Vanhorn   41
    The Language of Flowers   42

India through Windows
    Pull   45
    Through Windows
        Echoes   46
        Amber   46
        Le Meridien   47
        Walls   47
    Floating   48
    Dr. Meherjee's Widow   49
    The First Cut
        Figures of Eight   50
        Abed's Weight   51
        The First Cut   52
        Chrysanthemums   53
        Arcs   54

England
    Fitting In   57
    Looking for a House
        The Day the Birds Left   58
        Matthew's Dwelling   58
        Eating Winkles in Paignton   59
        Metonymy   59
        Inside the Frame   60
        Of Being Here   60
    Because the Land is Barren   61
    Echoes in Grey   62
    Shadows   66

Return to India
    Walking in a Lost Stanza
        Return   69
        Masquerade   70
        Held   71
        Ascent to Darjeeling   72
        Happy Valley   73
    Calcutta   74
    Grandmother's Teeth   75
    Ablution   76
    Birthday   77
    Age   78
    Watching through the Night   79
    In the First Wing-Strokes of Birds Searching   80
    When Mother Returns to India   81

*For Lucia,
because you have led me
to my muse.*

[Reif sind...]

Vorwärts aber und rückwarts wollen wir
Nicht sehn. Uns wiegen lassen, wie
Auf schwankem Kahne der See.

Friedrich Hölderlin

[The fruits are ripe...]

But we shall not look forward
Or back. Let ourselves rock, as
On a boat, lapped by the waves.

Friedrich Hölderlin
(translated by Richard Sieburth)

India from the Raj Bungalow

The Kingfisher

> *as if they were all one flesh, in a single dream,*
> *and nothing to make them true, but space, and time.*
> —John Burnside

The day the big pine fell, missing us by inches,
we watched the kingfisher's slow swirl
over the broken stump. Mutely, it worked a circle,
all afternoon in mother's eyes
as the sun came into the veranda floor.
If the railings stretched their length in silhouettes,
it would be winter.
      Light, then darkness inside the wafer thin walls
of pine; layers of exquisite wood-lace.
Our sheepdog ran to sniff at the termite-torn castle,
cocked a leg and went to look for the gecko we tried to tame
with milk and eggs under the rose trellis. And still
the blue flight as dusk flushes over the river.
Mother will paint this, I thought, in her mind at least,
even if she stopped painting when I was born. An exhaled 'o'
of breath as her eyes crinkle against the sun,
a breeze soft in her brown hair.

The timber people came from outside.
The gardeners wore grins
as they helped them roll the logs away.
All winter, they tended roses,
beds of *Bianca* and *Black Prince*, but this was
a windfall.
      The hole filled with shadows
in the dark. I willed the moon to show dancers
as it did always; there was no one. That night I dreamt
of roses caught in porcelain bowls, the scent elusive
in their maroon.

Hover

The deluge sudden over trees, mother in her housecoat running down the stairs to let the dogs in, telling everyone to hurry, hurry, or we get caught. My sister closes *Grey's Anatomy*, leans towards the river saying everything can wait; even *Ranikhet*. Mother slams windows shut, says hurry. Father's gaze on the river longs to stay.

Rain turns the lawns to brown pools of mud. We watch the river rise, the paper folding sound not registered till my sister says look, oh look; then it is the rustle of silk saris at a wedding. The sky turns green as the parrots fly by, so close we can see claws tucked up against white-feathered bellies.

Mother says hurry but we wait for the river dolphins. She can move tomorrow, or when the rain stops. The suitcases on the landing trip everyone up all day. At dusk, another snatch of green. It's a female high on a tree, its eyes closed, neck exposed as the blue-ringed male pulls its feathers free of rain. I watch father's hand loop in mother's hair.

Ranikhet: 'Queen's Garden' – a hill station in the Kumaon range of the Himalayas

Coalescence

> *A few more years, a few more ghosts to embrace*
> — Yusef Komunyakaa

Inside the Tate's turbine room, I am
sandwiched between dysfunctional machines.
Rain splatters glass. I thought my skin had forgotten
the sudden cleansing of the dive,
hands reaching for the floor of the pool
the CESC children swam in. Only us,
not outsiders who went down to the river.
Something here smells of coal. Gritty,
coated with coal dust, we were
told to bathe thrice daily, all summer.
We didn't recognize words in our mother tongues
confusing dirt with tint of skin. We were children
of the CESC, convent-educated,
playing in knee-socks and organdie dresses,
our days dotted with tennis matches
and rose walks, gardeners and maids'
brushes walloping brown lignite
off door-meshes in clouds.

Clouds that returned to powder our limbs
after each bath. We plunged into the pool,
making the powerhouse chimneys bob in surprise.
Where does the coal smell come from? We would swim
like tadpoles, our washed skins turning
browner in the sun. Mothers yelled from verandas:
'five more minutes' as Zareen stroked the water back.

I can hear it lap against the edge as she swims.
Seven-year-old Buba dives so hard from the top board,
her underwear floats away amidst our shouts;

she swims, her white chemise a scrap of sail.
A few more years and she will have it right.
Nothing keeps us from the pool; not frogs coming back
despite the increased bleaching powder;
not snakes, which nest under the deep-end stairs.
Our arms return to waves, a flail
toward the dark.

Tate: Tate Modern, London.
CESC: Calcutta Electric Supply Corporation, a thermal power station that used to belong to a British company.

My Father's Crown

1.

I don't know if I speak of you
Father, when you opened
your mouth, mother spoke out.
Your ears are tuned
to the power station's boiler room,
clamouring for attention. You
stride through the powerhouse
shouting orders. Soot-covered,
you are a king. When you return,
a dark shape in the deodar avenue,
dwarfed by chimneys,
our dogs bark a welcome
to the jingle of keys in the lock
I ignore.

2.

I ignore the voice in our bungalow
telling me why it is necessary
to chop down the frangipani bough
that thrusts through my window each day
with bouquets of white flowers.
Our father-daughter talk is blocked
when khaki-clad gardeners arrive
to lop off the branch
jammed in the window as I leave
for school. I return to a distanced tree
dripping its white sap
helplessly on the grass. You
say it is love, that silent seeping,
that you are trying to keep away snakes.

3.

You say you are trying to keep away snakes,
the day I put your slippers on,
mother nodding assent. You disappear
behind the newspaper article
about hoodlums stealing place-names.
I can see your defiant smile
as they begin to vanish -
paved stones carved with British names
from our deodar walk
snaking to the powerhouse. An old landmark,
your expression as you watch me
slip my feet inside your slippers,
thinking your daughter's feet fit and
what a small man you must be.

4.

What a small man you must be
sometimes. When mother switches off
the Cliff Richard tapes
and there's nothing left
to echo off my bedroom walls,
silence freezes around me
like an icicle; I am a shadow
drifting down the velvet tunnel
of your mute tongue,
swallowed by mother's reasons
that never ceased to make you
more silent, as if you had been
born tongue-less.
I have never asked how it feels.

5.

I have never asked how it feels
to be carried tall on someone's shoulders
a whole day when you are six,
worlds opening; in front of your eyes
a vista of trees winding somewhere
you would inhabit like a shadow.
On your brother's shoulders you are
a kestrel testing wings,
the avenue of deodars like a landing strip
I begged to take flight from. Your ears buzz
as the blue sky mingles with leaves
and weight drops away, your happiness
at such fever pitch it flies clear
out of hearing range.

6.

Clear out
of hearing range, a voice
telling me why writing will not work.
At seventeen, I cut my hair,
impatient for judgment
to trickle down to 'no'.
The maroon I wore
was for a similar reason, for lack
of narrative thread. You never told me
when the connection went,
memories of treks, pony rides.
I drifted away like a balloon,
romancing gaps; calling home
with fewer words each time.

7.

Calling home with fewer words each time,
Didi kept the banyan tree a secret;
its dark roots drenched in dew, its hollows
where something grew,
new skin swelling like a waxing moon.
She never talked of her first love.
The summer Didi left,
we lay on a hillside in Musoorie,
cursing you. That's the first
I saw you cry, curled on grass
as if you had taken root . We looked on
with dreamer's eyes,
our blue-brown gaze torching the crater
rim of your black eyes.

8.

Lost in your black-cratered eyes:
Red Road and the Strand,
horses in the rear-view mirror
poised over the highest bar, frozen
in my memory as we move away
from the school where I was
to be captain. The perfect balance
found one summer on a see-saw,
that record of my life floating,
a dot in the mirror.
You swallowed my life when you returned
to rule the old power plant. Don't
spew up place names, hoping
to bring me back.

9.

As if you hoped to bring sound back
whole from the doctor's office,
I saw you absorb an echo.
They shone a tiny light in your ear
and you became a hole. Machines resonated
with sounds of long vowels
sliding past your throat. I could feel
your fear sucking in a world
it could not reproduce. Mother's battery
of questions did not reveal
that you held that world captive; or how
your hand reached for something
unyielding in the dark machine room
and hovering, you found me.

10.

And you found me hovering
on your shoulder
when I was three, blue sleeves
of my best party dress wings
in the breeze. I touched ground
to take off. Everybody stared, even
gardeners and day labourers. Officers smiled
as you bore me on your arm
through the canopy of deodar trees
all the way to the power-plant.
Through the din and smoke,
offerings started to appear;
bowls of fluffed rice like frangipani
blossoms. You could make magic.

11.

Magic, this too:
how you never came home until the sun was
a zero in the sky haloed by light,
and the dogs hoarse with barking. You said
life was facts and figures. Four
equal sides in our family, each absolute,
a wall impervious to change
until one left. Then we took turns
as hypotenuse for the opposed
to lean on. You never saw
the kingfisher swirling over pines
or the river swelling with rain. Fact is,
the siren was wailing as you walked home
at sixty unable to talk of emotion.

12.

Even at sixty unable to talk of emotion,
when you came home I was
too far away to see the small shadow
returning through the deodar path.
I can't hide that I have walked out on you
since then, yet how I miss the meadow of bees
buzzing behind your mouth's dam. You
won't fight the head of hair
disappearing from photos, dark
before its release. Were you there
when the owl that mother had freed
returned to my frangipani bough at night
as if it didn't know where to go? Weight is
an inheritance, like the shape of eyes.

13.

An inheritance, this eye-
shaped lake at the end of summer
gloomy with pine,
where a forest fire stretching like a snake
made flying foxes appear in the air,
by magic. You said
you could not sleep; your eyes open
through owls' hoots and the moon's arcing
to dawn, red wreathing through the rim
of hills like a wing. My child's eye holds
the flame of azaleas in your palm,
mother humming
beside a pile of gingham napkins
as if something were going to happen.

14.

As if something were going to happen,
your black-cratered eyes tried
to sign a warning
clear as *keep away from snakes.*
I wouldn't hear from my room
in the bungalow, mother and you
stranded as though on two sides of a lake,
emotion withdrawn out of range
like a wreath on water, your face
hoping to bring it back, find mother
humming in the kitchen.
But inheritance is
a small man returning home
with fewer words each time.

Behind this Eye

You come on your Yezdi,
knees pointing
in two directions. The 'V'
of your shirt signifies:
dusk is a mantle
on your shoulders,
my arms are around you
on the bike, engine throbbing
like heartbeat. *Hold on*,
but we are off.

****

Inside my window
between the wire mesh
and the metal grill
a red-cheeked bulbul pair
have nested. You pass
my old place you say
and sigh.

****

Where does this one
come from,
clutching with its windows?
Like someone else's dreams
I will inhabit.

****

On my birthday,
a photo of the bougainvillea tree,
its mauve flowers
on my art deco blouse,
trailing up the stone wall.

****

On the bench
where we twine
our arms together,
look: a letter.

****

The house had grilled windows
which sent away the river.
Morning ferried school children
to the other side,
their voices,
their hands dipping in water.
Gentle ripples on shore
two lawns away.

****

We played with the Russian doll
in grandmother's cupboard
on Sundays. You took its head,
I, its stiff skirt,

You pulled
another head off and I
a skirt, until we had
a line of faces
on your side, skirts on mine
like soldiers going to war.

★★★★

In all your paintings there is
a bird that hovers
over cliff tops and pine trees
or wisps of smoke
that wane
away in the sky.

★★★★

I too have dwelled
in sad places. The old banyan tree
at school that made the dark
look brown. I could hardly bear
to look at it, the fingers
rooted everywhere, the holes
in its trunk where things lived.
Its immense shade.

★★★★

If I say 'I', I become
your grey mufti
or a maroon tie.
A walk by the flower stalls
near West End, a café
while it pours with rain.
Your steps on the stairs,
your dark brown eyes and
where was I?

Shining Diamond

to Varun

This will remain;
the tar-grey parade ground
stretched to alabaster walls,
insistent traffic dodging night.

We perch on stone steps,
await 'insti's
flickering lights to turn on
as a guitar strums the chords

distinctly in the seminal quiet:
wish you were here.
The long wait for dawn,
when your mind stoked with the Floyd

can vault the wall to the other side,
where the first trees are
green-gold and smoke-hazy.

Insti: *short for 'institution'; the Armed Forces Medical College canteen.*

Subtracted Memory

After Silko

The Hopi can disappear into jagged-faced rocks in the middle of plains and quiet pools waving with wild watercress. They can disappear – a generation or two, a family grazing sheep on a still autumn's day – into four-petalled squash-flower or cottonwood tree. They can loop between times, from 'now' to 'not now'; fill their stories with wide-open mouths of clock-swallowing arroyos. The only constant: space: earth, the mother that waits to claim blood and bone back to loam. That is what you wished for, constancy like a star; timeless belonging. Like survival in AFMC which herds exceptions into flocks of junkies who sink into stellar visions, who flunk each year; which weeds from each batch the rough-edged gift, all that does not fit. *The difference is*

in power; you say, licking mayo off your burger, *the difference between D. P. S. and Mt. St. Mary's*. I am perched on a bike in *Jaws*, where there is no un-belonging, where people smoke hash and laugh over sex-jokes on a notice board, negotiate 'well preserved' things: Yamahas, Enfields, Moments. There, I, inside the void, in a bomb-like contentment. You, in the margin, eyebrows raised for someone has said again: *you sing beautifully*. You are unaware of bringing back a memory of love, singing like you do. A pause, then lights,
            emotion,
              action:
cymbals, drum, electric guitar throbbing for a cue.
              Then you,

on the plateau, singing as the first drops spill. Khanna curled into Reshmi's knee, feigning love; another Kapoor. Reshmi another me, feigning. *Yin and Yang*. I lean over your knee to cover your guitar. Don't take it away; this moment will sustain.

A wall of rain as I race home on my motorbike, you perched on the back wheel. I didn't intend to come out of the bathroom and find you changing. Thank me when I take you home *beyond the call of duty*, when I rev, and leave you rooted on the parade ground. The story isn't about belonging anymore. *Please*

go, you say, *please understand*. Here comes your mother after the accident. She will hold you while the night stars; and you slip back to St. Mary's, the school that can reproduce *Nights in White Satin*. The last we meet – *just once; please* – we don't know it is the last time. You thrust a picture of God into my hands as you leave; *you need it*, you say; then, *let me go, or I will be no different from them*. The Hopi know a different belonging. A tension as we totter, pulled taut like breath sucked in. Then you vanish with the rest, into a squash-flower, its petals pointing everywhere at the promise of night pooling over the parade ground

walls,

where cattails wave.

A.F.M.C.: *Armed Forces Medical College;*
D. P. S.: *Delhi Public School;*
Mt. St. Mary's: *A school.*

Little Death

When he arrives it is 5.20 p.m.:
Manhattan's skyline stacked in shades of sunset.
His suitcase circles a whining carousel.
After the long flight, his undecided legs
wobble between Immigration and Customs;
his mind a twelve-hour fog
of voices straining to split a chord.

The taxi driver points out Brooklyn Bridge.
His eyes hunt Times Square's lights,
kneaded-ice-cream parlours,
Starbucks at every street corner.
U.S.A. is déjà vu;
a clothesline on a balcony taut in the breeze.
He will find her behind one of the doors
of this infinite prospect: buildings
with their tops out of sight. He arrives,
pulling his suitcase into the unfamiliar
room, where dusk is a line of starlings.

In the New World

Immigrants

> *The load would have to be lightened*
> — Suzanne Cleary

First of all, stillness; the hum of a tuning fork
escalating to silence. The past
scars like an icicle. In the new country
you acquire new skin; Mexican;

the 'j' in your name quietened.
Some things must lose significance;
everyone knows it will be necessary
to throw out father's magic

mercury-vapour lamp moonlighting a room.
Necessary to exorcise the scent of oranges
in winter afternoons on the veranda;
old definitions of words we loved so much,

like 'foreign'. Mother's painting covered in dust
hangs behind the shoe rack.

Split

I

The yellow balloons were dancing against windows
as we drove away after the wedding,
everyone crying, even my sister
who had apologised for not being able to.
Vines and flowers swathed everywhere,
we quoted Ezekiel and Elizabeth Browning
under a trellised arch that threw a net of shadows
on our faces. My father-in-law cut down the leaves.
Everybody and their dogs welcomed me
to the family. Tuesday dinners at Grandma's
followed Sunday washing at Mom's.
Two more weddings the same year and
I in front of the mirror
throwing handfuls of clothes on the bed;
the white, then the blue with the hat,
low and high heels, silk scarves.
Even my parents forgot I hadn't always been
a part of the other family. Across continents,
letters filled with news of dinners, dog fights,
the length of Jake's runs, a cousin stuck
dumbfounded in Kuwait as troops lit Iraq
like the fourth of July.

II

Now, we cut the cake – *click* – now we raise glasses –
click – group photos please:
your mom and dad smiling through tears,
grandparents in a row,
there is cousin Reshmi
with her first smile after the break,
the *justice of the peace* who gave us a time-piece,
Didi in her see-through chiffon
and you with your hair dishevelled,
hesitant face lit up; there's you Jake,

riven from the group,
from your mother's sap green dress.

III

I hadn't known there were
so many Christian factions,
Lutheran, Apostolic,
a Mennonite great-aunt in floral frock
resonant of our wedding quilt,
a missionary cousin in Japan
with seven girls in pig tails and
a boy.

She sets each night
on your pillow, Mom –
the girl who wants to run away
while you fidget
with toothbrush and soap
in the new bathroom.

IV Grandma's Death

Music
make me feel
the pew she leaves
three rows away

the press of melody
in unfamiliar voices

grandpa's mouth
open like a door.

Bluebill

to Jake

He mock-raises his electric-blue cone of martini
as if a sea, the bottles of *Absolut* behind him
arranged carefully. The bartender's cap
is blue. Bill
         has struck a lode and now I know
what you did not say – the 90-degree day
and how you found him waiting
by the hand-drawn *Bass*.

I too have seen the star-breasted bird
build daily on the clematis. He plucks out
twigs and bits of grass, like tunes.
My dark robin, if you could sing

I can guess what pierced note
would stain your throat.

Vanhorn

Not him –
the others were moving in the photos,
each delivering hand become three
out of focus hands
linked by veins of light –

he remained still.
Behind him drawn blinds, a violin

by the window. He had had enough;
even his old shirt flails from the hook –
it will get rid of men who go
with slaps on the back –

look at the hyphen
of his mouth, zipped
against words.

The Language of Flowers

to Kathryn

Your green note this May:
gourds on the window
arched behind violets;

startled birds-of-paradise
on a table full of bills
and unopened letters;

under the magnolia tree, Nancy
with her hair unfurled;
you tell me how

the red-bud blooms.

India through Windows

Pull

The room I check into has tall windows
framing the branches of a giant gulmohar
that beckons in the breeze. I am thrilled
until the tide of 3 a.m. traffic spills in,
a fusillade of horns and strange dogs' yapping.
The watchman wakes and bangs his stick
on my door, telling me to turn off
the porch light. I can't sleep for mosquitoes
that buzz and settle on my skin, like memories
of a family I saw here, bent acute, arms waving
between sheaves of grain; of a tree-full of parrots
released from gravity.

Through Windows

I. Echoes

Dust here is
a disease   It returns
like a cloud through windows
coats the bed posts   a feathered thing
on the back of chairs

On the streets people
carry soil on their feet
You leave
your slippers outside my door
but bear the world in

II. Amber

The old path is memory
At tea we stroll down
the rose walk   buds
on the tips of our scissors

They pour cement
to seal the half-names
on the pavestones
Look at it slip
down our backs

III. Le Meridien

There was a bookshop
in the foyer   the smell of coffee
very new   I could forget
the proximity of trains
the hotel's light
carried on their backs

Your rawhide slippers
are webs   In the dark you draw
arcs with your arm
connecting distances
a mime of how time passes

IV. Walls

Poona is Tuscan now
but I remember Coffee House in gilt
and cream on my first date
Mucha's *Les Saisons*
on walls   like prophecies
and trolleys full of alphonso
mangoes outside
the plump orange melting
down our tongues

Inside this town
are bones that give
a bit more each time

Floating

The Victorian railings say it all:
hammock stretched tight, a tension as you sway,
pulling on a string. Paradoxes,
Danesh, how you would laugh
that moustache-curling laugh
that always drew women into your life.
I need to deflect my hunger

with *batasas* from Dorabjee
and your lemon-mint tea;
to stand on Wadia rail bridge
as the six-o'clock to Bombay rushes by.
You are in the doldrums,
pulled by the *Mutha* dragging into the dam.
The 'projects' spring up,
roots sunk deeper in eroding soil.
You watch the ebbing woods,

hoping for an interruption –
a call from Malini perhaps
from somewhere yet else – that would cut
the waiting; the drowning *Mutha*.

Batasa: a biscuit
Mutha: a river in Poona.

Dr. Meherjee's Widow

She cackles at us, blowing smoke through her old teeth. Her little-girl hair is damp. She stares at the Discovery channel.

Dr. Meherjee's widow has a cockatoo. That is why we are here. Danesh moves towards the bedroom door. The cry is of a bird of prey; it claws at bars. Danesh yells as he comes back held in talons. The widow's fingers curl as something tears across the screen, a magnificent ripple of life chasing, so beautiful you don't want it to stop even though you know what it means. '*Don't* bring her out.'

It was a gift from a patient, Danesh explains in the bedroom. It is an old lady's room: canopied bed; smell of talcum powder. I look at the photo, mind darting to grandmother's fan, the folded quills. A cage swings in the balcony, suspended in Danesh's eyes. I know he thinks of Homi; the asylum of his laugh. The cockatoo whispers, its soft down fluttering. I edge towards the door.

The bird cry rips the room; Dr. Meherjee's widow screaming '*Don't*.' Her fingers close around a cigarette, a seared hiss from its live eye. Suddenly the air is feathered.

The First Cut

> *endless turning and returning . . .*
> *endless attempts at restitution*
> — Andrej Warminski

I FIGURES OF EIGHT

She will dive into this unknown
longitude, where the sky is a sea,
where houses, farms have locked in blue,
transparent in a trick of light.

She will drift on this tide
returning him,
its undertow visible
like a hand through porcelain,

pulling her to a background
like an old movie
where the dancers are
intent as bees.

II Abed's Weight

I wouldn't have known you,
you say, with a waist-long beard,
skin burnt black as you slaved.

Palestine – the word burns
holes in your eyes, but you laugh
about the history that leaves;

how I find you flushed with sun,
sporting a belly. Something gone
from your face when I call out

brother.
When my arms find you,
they won't hold weight.

III The First Cut

This little girl wants to dance.
Her feet under the bright green skirt
already beat a rhythm. The other
children know this dance
and hop in front of the idol,
their *sarees* and *dhotees* slipping.

We wait for the drummers
in a Chicago schoolroom,
where at first I felt
a sharp pain in finding myself
alone. You can never know
what will rip you.

The air electric
as drummers arrive,
sticks poised over waiting drums.
The first cut
makes petals shower;

the new wives undulate,
lamps and conch-shells in hands,
their faces blooming.
The little girl has a flower in her hand,

has offered it to the man
who made her feet belong.

IV Chrysanthemums

Chrysanthemums were my eyes
as a child, turned to a window.
They were resilient, going without
water, till you remembered.
For seventeen years they looked
at green garage doors, for nothing moved
where I grew up.

Chrysanthemum petals arch
like cats
before letting the sun out.
You once said
the bald head when the petals fell,
was edible.

V Arcs

The papaya-seller's hips sway in eights
as she moves up
to empty her basket of fruit.

Calangute beach is drowsing,
light disappeared in holes
behind shut eyes.

Leaping towards me,
this fragmented sound
that says 'catch.'

Calangute Beach: a beach in Goa

England

Fitting In

> *You in thin air*
> — Amanda Dalton

The old swing taut under the bay tree,
you pull out of the frame,
aching to leave that square of grass.
Before you fit in, the tree will go.
At the snip of scissors,
memory returns from nowhere,
one about the girls' dresses
beating in the breeze.

Balance is what perches
after sweeps through air. For a moment
you are in no man's land with birds,
but something tugs you back.
Feel your feet back on earth;
the edges of this photo tear
like festoons from a boat.

Looking for a House

1. THE DAY THE BIRDS LEFT

This memory in sepia:
over the bridge, a sky filled with birds,
their intense chatter as they soar
out of hearing.

Your hand
curled around my fingers
on our last drive; pain
become an 'o'.

2. MATTHEW'S DWELLING

He wants to share
this 1930's council house,
full of solid things – bakelite
switches, mahogany furniture.

Evening a cobweb
over photos on a chest
of drawers, as his own smile
tries too, to coax him
from corners. But someone left

the window open
and speedwells have gathered
in his blue eyes.

3. Eating Winkles in Paignton

Because the sea takes them back
these small ones are
crawling away from me,
filling the sand with ellipses.

The green barnacle hastening back
to the wave that leaves
upturned limpets on the ground,
clams, crabs, slugs, a fringe

of weed, is part of here, this being,
turning dark like the girl in green.
My teeth close
on small things the sea brought in.

4. Metonymy

Not everything
lost to distance: the girl
running to waves,

unafraid of losing
her balance to the sea
inside her whelk ears.

5. Inside the Frame

You must have known
I would trawl for the small ones
that don't matter if they escape,

these small-fish records
of summer, your skin
absorbing dusk as we blend

in the flux of perception.
This frame is an inheritance;
a palimpsest of nets

behind eyes caught in the photo.

6. Of Being Here

For you who don't know
why I am: look

at the infinity of Matthew's
lorry carrying bales of hay

as it weaves past
trees, the bees seeking

inside foxgloves, patterns
of crops or blend of claret light

on fields immersed in celandine,
a heifer licking a calf's honey skin.

Because the Land is Barren

As though it were his aorta he plucks at,
the *rababa* a pulse at his groin,

a nomad tweaking out a muse
from the lute on his thigh;

melody that won't need
more than the lone string

to accompany his desert song.

Echoes in Grey

I

The man I remember
walks staccato past flower vendors
and Marz-O-Rin
where couples poise ice-cream
livid with cherries.
I follow quickly,
the street marked
with grey all the way
to my room,

where I am drawn to scent
of mango blossoms filling the air.
He leans in his chair,
his legs splayed. He is bad
he says, at words;
but our feet can speak.
I at his feet,
making colt's eyes.

II

All day long the neighbour's mare
has nickered in fields.
I try appeasing her with apples,
but she runs away,
nuzzling air. There is nothing
I can do, see how she gallops
bullet straight; half beats
like echoes. She looks back,
startled to see who follows,
but there's no shadow there.

III

At night the mare is
a wave in the field,
her cremello foal nosing
where her mother's tail
beckons like a whip.

IV

The south-clouds have blended
the mare grey. She is
invisible in shadow;
a flame in light.

I watch her appear
and disappear, hooves whipping
iris and purple heather.

She changes shape,
out-distancing hedgerows,
becomes the scent of rain.

Shadows

After Lee Harwood

This morning a fall
of chestnuts   a hard leaving
this rain of consonants   your eyes
crushed frangipani
or shadows on the river

At night that dark square
absorbs your neighbour's windows blinking
in the silence you bring back   bird call and
wings on trees
drawing your fleur-de-lys
curtain   even stillness holds

a leaving you know
in your arms   a shadow
of hair or a green silk blouse
a tea garden in Darjeeling when you were

a boy   hill smoke
or a wisp of grey from ashtray to mirror
you say I leave
things behind   your eyes by the window
nickel coins on a child's loin
strung on a thin black thread

Return to India

Walking in a Lost Stanza

to Srijoy

RETURN

Laughing, trying to find breath again,
we meander through groups of pedestrians,
cyclists, rickshaw-pullers, taxis,
blind with memory. You steer
with one arm, people, cows, dustbins,
umbrellas, shops, lurching into view.
You say you are drunk, tell me
to roll the window down and swear,

swear at the world
a stream vibrating from chest
and head, of blown out breath;
of rain.

MASQUERADE

In the confusion of arrival, the resonance of your footsteps inside my tympanic bones, lost these six years. You lead me as if to mask the entrance of other selves:

a woman transformed with summer; a man departed to a different view.

Held

A fall of fruit
marking our lope beside empty buildings,
here I am allowed, in childhood,
in sleep, to imagine histories joined;
your feet beside ours.

Sister and I knew our way
to that forbidden window, open
to mango leaves sweeping in,
the blossoms a haunting,
a green smell within closed doors
that did not leave
until our fingers released
handfuls of cloth over thighs;
a caress of ghosts in frocks
that locked us in,
as if they would never let us stray.

Ascent to Darjeeling

Mohuagong and Gompa arrive
with a rush of cooler air. After that
memory: the sharp scent
of *Goodricke* tea in winter afternoons.

Nathmull's where the jagged brim of road
throws one against windows,
each hairpin bend returning weight
as the valley starts to float in air.

Before we reach the toy train
at Ghoom, a young girl with braids
in ribbons; the thread
of *Margaret's Hope*.

'Goodricke', 'Nathmull's' and 'Margaret's Hope' are tea estates.

Happy Valley

Decayed bungalows,
fruit trees
pull into your voice,
flotsam
from your belonging
in fragments
of Nepalese
as you talk
with your cousins
in the taxi.
I had forgotten
how one returns
to the hollow
of a hand.

Calcutta

An old meaning in this fragment,
where elders at a wedding
have found words
in a flutter of hand- fans;

words that always seemed to halt
and pulse in thin throats,
hesitant to reveal visions
of the old city; this

sudden moon ascending.

Grandmother's Teeth

After the operation, she insists
that the attendant is wrong:
her teeth were not removed
while she slept, but still
in water on the bathroom shelf

at home. I remember her
on the wooden bench on the balcony,
bougainvilleas flowering
behind her, the sky
wide over rooftops where
dusk has brought a shoal of clouds.
When the ice cream vendor tolls a bell
and plants his box on the street corner,
children will arrive like magic.

Perhaps that is what she had wished to say
when she named
our childhood the best time
in her life. If a tide beckons
beyond the coast of teeth,
her breath will follow, trusting.

Ablution

When grandmother died,
the skeletal being
drifting behind our eyes
as we opened her door,
also seemed to leave. We looked
at her moorings, our hands
diving between cushions on her sofa,
into a draw string bag, arrested
by pad and pen, a fan
we tied up again, left
with a promise to feel
that caress of water.

Birthday

As if he heard a voice remind him
from the next room, grandfather felt
he was going to turn a hundred
a day before his birthday. The flat silent,
dusk suffusing curtains,
he sent the maid hurrying to the bazaar
for sweets for a celebration.

We said we didn't know how he got it wrong,
arrived a whole day before his time
to that lifelong urgency;
his self in the green tweed suit,
who answered as if a guest had appeared,
blowing through the hollow of a conch shell
the sound of sea.

Age

I think of birds. Daily his fingers float
through static, turn knobs on the radio
next to his 1920s' haircut.
His hand that can still perform,
can find his glasses. The inverted newspaper
leans on a pillow, but his eye is confident
of spinning back the world
right way up again. He will not hang
like a bat from some dark wall, is able
to steer his hundred year old day
alone. We must let him fly.

Watching through the Night

The road I envision is a black line
pulling my grandfather's carriage
to gates that lock as if to dam a river
I will find, waking. A watchman's call
arcs through windows: 'watch through the night'.

I see his young face lit by gaslight,
the wheels of his carriage; a cobbled road
wet with rain. I know where he goes;

an arm holding a lantern by a gate
has formed a moon, an eye
inside me that won't close.

In the First Wing-strokes of Birds Searching

Jasmine sellers with fragrant loads
on their backs, their chant a rhythm of feet
on the way to the flower market
under Howrah Bridge. An old Calcutta
by the river, Princep Ghat and Fairley Place
sleepy in the first wing-strokes
of birds searching in the wake of boats.

Our grandparents' world
beyond the familiar; this everyday,
awakening. Places I have heard of,
Murshidabad's porous palaces,
battle fields of Plassey, a ghostly contour
thinning towards the end of vision. The beginning
of the tale invisible; a fugitive prince
fleeing to refuge in the night. There,
behind the receding dark, a koel's call of rain.

When Mother Returns to India

Life is a palimpsest
— Andy Brown

There was no water in the fishpond by the time I was born, only a ring of stones. Our mothers hissed if they caught us by the pond's edge, looking down at pebbles that looked like birds' eggs. Small fish darted in the water we imagined, flashes of goldfish near the bottom, tadpoles and black mollies; fish of our making we called 'dark angels'. I could almost see the legendary carp turn from the edge; shadow arcing.

We said we couldn't see the fish because they hid. It was camouflage, like a lizard soaked up by the sun or flurries melting on my black wool cape, which pulls in the wind now that I have let it out of photos where mother is always wearing it. She looks gay in black and white, her eyebrows thick in England; wings at the sides of her laughing eyes.

When mother returns to India, the trees have turned green. It is as if a season is lost. She sits by the fishpond, her dreams tinged with boatmen's songs floating through the wrought iron fence. Fins turn the light; her eyes indigo with a kingfisher's flight from the pine under her window. She folds her cape inside out in a drawer, the red lining straining to hold the press of dark wings I will inherit. Our parents churn up pebbles on the river-walk with their feet on nights that conceive us. Imagine a night silvered by moon, an owl's hoot piercing a question; answers carrying from swing to swing on a breeze.

I don't remember water in the fishpond. My first memory is of the sitting room carpet rushing out to meet lawns. I gaze at the inexplicable expanse opening up beyond wire-meshed doors, greens rolling down to surging river, an ocean to me. I can almost feel the ancient gills spread and close like a lady's fan; the bird-like shadow.

www.ingramcontent.com/pod-product-compliance
Lightning Source LLC
Chambersburg PA
CBHW030048100426
42734CB00037B/610